Your Complete Forecast 2018 Horoscope

GEMINI

Your Complete Forecast 2018 Horoscope

GEMINI

BEJAN DARUWALLA
With
NASTUR DARUWALLA

Ranvir Books
HARPER element

First published in India in 2017 by Harper Element
An imprint of HarperCollins *Publishers*

P-ISBN: 978-93-5277-334-3
E-ISBN: 978-93-5277-335-0

2 4 6 8 10 9 7 5 3 1

HarperCollins *Publishers*
A-75, Sector 57, Noida, Uttar Pradesh 201301, India
1 London Bridge Street, London, SE1 9GF, United Kingdom
2 Bloor Street East, Toronto, Ontario M4W 1A8, Canada
Lvl 13, 201 Elizabeth Street (PO Box A565, NSW, 1235), Sydney
NSW 2000, Australia
195 Broadway, New York, NY 10007, USA

Typeset in 11.5/15 Sabon
By Saanvi Graphics, Noida

Printed and bound at
MicroPrints (India), New Delhi

Contents

Special Message from Bejan and Nastur 6

Monthly Round-up 14

Weekly Review
(By Phases of the Moon) 17

Achievements 2018 69

Body Language 71

Colours of Life 74

Important Dates 76

Secret of Life 79

Success Secret of No. 17 81

World Horoscope 2018 84

Salute and Tribute 88

About the Author 93

Important Announcement 95

GEMINI

22 May–22 June

Geminis are kings of contacts and communication. They reach out to people and places everywhere, including the Milky Way and the immense galaxies and spaces. That's their speciality.

- **Colours:** Blue, yellow, yellow-orange
- **Colours that promotes love, romance and social harmony:** Sky blue
- **Colours that promote earning power:** Grey, silver
- **Gems:** Agate, aquamarine
- **Metal:** Quicksilver
- **Scents:** Lavender, lilac, lily of the valley

- **Quality:** Mutability (= flexibility)
- **Quality most needed for balance:** Thought that is deep rather than superficial
- **Strongest virtues:** Great communication skills, quickness and agility of thought, ability to learn quickly
- **Deepest need:** Communication
- **Characteristics to avoid:** Gossiping, hurting others with harsh speech, superficiality, using words to mislead or misinform
- **Day:** Wednesday
- **Number:** Five
- **Flowers:** Lavender, blue violet, lily of the valley

- **Trees:** Hazel, chestnut and all nut-bearing trees
- **Foods:** Nuts and all vegetables grown above the ground, except cabbage, are foods associated with Gemini, as are such herbs and spices as marjoram, caraway and aniseed

SPECIAL MESSAGE FROM BEJAN AND NASTUR

You must take care of your health and finances. On the positive side, expect promotions, better work opportunities, happy relationships with pets, servants and colleagues. Care in food and regular exercise will be the secret to a happy comfortable life. I am sure you smart Geminis will get it right.

Geminis are changeable and often moody. Their symbol, the twins, means they are often at odds with themselves – the mind demanding one thing, the heart demanding the opposite. This in turn manifests as two very different people. As a Gemini's significant other, you might reach a point where you wonder which twin you are with.

JUPITER

For you intelligent Geminis I have worked out a threefold plan. The first plan will be about the focus of Jupiter in your sixth angle. This focus will be on colleagues and servants, health, food, shelter and all matters related to the necessaries of life. Except earlier job opportunities and services including even freelancing or doing handy jobs as they say or just supervising on workers will be of immense importance and purpose. Also, relatives and friends who rely upon you, pets, in fact all animals will help to shape your destiny to a great extent.

The second part of the plan is about finding your own self. By helping others, taking care of your health, innovating new systems of work, making work sound like fun and joy and being consistent and steady on the work level you will achieve much. You Geminis are brilliant but fickle, ever-changing and easily bored. That will not do now.

Lastly, please do not take matters lightly but accept your responsibility willingly and happily. Do not be sarcastic and argue over petty matters. Have a broad mind and vast mental horizon. Sometimes you Geminis lose confidence and become defensive. Therefore, I am assuring you again and again to not only overcome all obstacles but also do great and grand work.

SATURN

The two main planets I take are Jupiter and Saturn. Saturn will be in your eighth angle from 21 December 2017 to 22 March 2020. To put it simply, the eighth angle stands for taxes, loans, joint finance, inheritance, legacy, lottery, public funds and trusts, and handling very specially the funds and money of others, accidents, rebirth, great spiritual powers, tantra and mantra. But the real contradiction is that the eighth house stands for very good and noble deeds, as well as evil deeds like rape, murder, loot, arson, blackmail. You Geminis are very intelligent, exceptionally sharp. This intelligence can be used both ways. Luckily in 2018, Saturn in your eighth house and Jupiter in your sixth house are in a very fine and powerful position astrologically. Therefore, you will get both honey and money. The possible months for it are January, March, May, July (specially), September, November. Just for your information I am giving you the other features connected with the eighth house: marital status of a woman, longevity, death, obstacle, disgrace, defeat, misery, loss of memory, killing a living being, capital punishment, nature of death, place of death, wickedness, father's indebtedness, deviation from expected norms, frightful place, difficult route, crevices, finding faults, humiliation, wife's wealth, sudden unexpected gains, hidden talents, spiritual pursuits and attainments, son of an elder sister.

Obviously, all of these cannot happen. But you Geminis are very curious and therefore very specially for you I am exerting a little more and giving you all the possible information. I always take into very active consideration the outer planets, Pluto, Neptune and Uranus.

URANUS

Uranus is the planet of revolution and evolution. Therefore, you will make strange friends and acquaintances. Eccentric and intelligent people could form a group for you. The strange and mysterious effects of Uranus may be felt in February, June, August, October and December.

NEPTUNE

In 2018, Neptune remains in your angle of profession, business, parents, in-laws, prestige and power. Neptune is also superbly placed with Saturn and Pluto. Therefore, funds for any type of work or entertainment or marriage or films or events should be available. I have just invented a special phrase for you. The great car Rolls Royce also rolls on money. Let me put it all in a different way. The real year for starting an enterprise or expanding a business or having a wish-fulfilment in life is 2018. The real spin-off will be in 2019.

PLUTO

Pluto holds hands with Saturn in your eighth angle. I never command and give orders. I believe in 'Live and let live'. But if you believe in God or Mother Nature you should most certainly worship your chosen energy and power in 2018 carefully. It helps. It will protect you against evil vibrations and help you in doing good deeds. I repeat that this is only my humble suggestion. You are welcome to your own beliefs and opinions. Just for your information I am pointing out that the holy days of prayers are Fridays, Saturdays and Thursdays.

MERCURY

I am sure most of you know that your main planet is Mercury. Mercury is the communication and contacts expert of the entire zodiac. We can conquer the whole world by messages and news and views. We know all about mobile, iPad, tablets, Internet and so on. Mercury will be in your own sign from 30 May to 12 June 2018. It will work wonders for you again from 1 to 17 February, 29

June to 5 September, 22 September to 9 October, 12 December to 4 January 2019, 9 January to 24 February 2019. Again, royally favourable from 27 June to 18 July, 14 September to 2 October 2019. And again from 9 December to 28 December. It will be easier for you to get your work done speedily and happily during the periods mentioned above. I want you to use it wisely and well, so that you and all your friends get the most out of it. But please remember that I am not God and astrology at best is only a guideline. Confidence is half the battle and astrology the other half. Perhaps the colours yellow, lemon, white can be both lucky and joyous for you Geminis.

MONTHLY ROUND-UP

January: Money, honey, riches, beautification, augmentation of income, good food, jewellery;

February: Research, contacts, communication, correspondence, brothers, sisters, relatives;

March: Home, house, property, renovation, decoration, alteration;

April: Love, romance, children, relationships, hobbies, sports;

May: Health, pets, servants, job, hygiene, colleagues;

June: Love, marriage, divorce, journeys, reaching out to people, also separations and lawsuits;

July: Joint finances, funds, loans, legacy, family issues and problems;

August: Sweet-and-sour relationships, publicity, conferences and meets, inspirational and intuitive moves and manoeuvres;

September: Prestige, status, power struggle, perks, new ventures and means of communication;

October: Socializing, group activities, marriage, love affair, happiness, laughter, the goodies of life;

November: Secret activities, health expenses, visits to hospitals, welfare centres, medical check-ups;

December: Fulfilment, happiness, money, marriage, confidence.

HAPPINESS QUOTA: 78 per cent

WEEKLY REVIEW (BY PHASES OF THE MOON)

2 JANUARY: FULL MOON IN CANCER

It's a start that is not at all flashy, yet there is an upsurge in certain spheres. All things related to money – funds, joint finance, the buying/selling/renting/leasing of property or house, even travel and documentation. A wide range to choose from. You'll have to be business-like and practical, and temporarily shelve both family matters and merrymaking.

8 JANUARY: LAST QUARTER IN LIBRA

There will be a fair amount of buying and selling of property, goods, even documents and papers that will form part of your work. Other than that, those in publicity-related fields too will be more than busy, but now domestic matters will jostle for space in your mind. Travel too, or even a shift to another place for work, or perhaps for study and research, is very likely.

17 JANUARY: NEW MOON IN CAPRICORN

It's more of the same, i.e., the focus will be more on work than anything else but now is the time to put your marvellous ability to get on with people, to empathize, communicate to good use. You might even make a career of it – social work, helplines, solace to the challenged, or just a 'chat show'. All of these will yield both pleasure, profit, interest. And sustained interest is something that you can be low on.

24 JANUARY: FIRST QUARTER IN TAURUS

Work finally takes a back seat as you sing '*I want to break free*' into the arms of a lover, a romantic affair, or soul vibes with your mate/partner. It's a time when creativity is at white heat for you. Hobbies, the arts, music will attract you to at least appreciate and enjoy, if not perform and excel at. Homemaking skills will also find you at your best.

31 JANUARY: FULL MOON IN LEO

The twin themes of finance and family will continue to dominate as a trend for February, but there are higher aspirations in the picture as well. These could take the form of travel, distant connections (I mean to far-off places), advanced study and research, opportunities to make a lot of money very fast. Ganesha says, no rash moves please, Geminis.

7 FEBRUARY: LAST QUARTER IN SCORPIO

The tinkle of money in the coffers is sweet music to anyone's ears. Even mine. For you, Geminis, it's a made-to-order situation for finances, deals, carefully made speculation. You may be flush with funds but going on a shopping binge, as you'd like to do, should be weighed against putting by for a rainy day. Creativity, higher study, children are all highlighted too.

15 FEBRUARY: NEW MOON IN AQUARIUS

The daredevilry and rashness of your sign comes to the fore. Wild gambles, a killing on the stock market, dangerous sports like Grand Prix or Formula One racing – you're truly flirting with life and death. The only advice Ganesha bids me to give you is check your goals, your temper, and your spending. This whole forecast applies to love and romance too. You might wind up being involved with the wrong person.

23 FEBRUARY: FIRST QUARTER IN GEMINI

It's as if you've been feeling your oats last week, and will now meekly accept the bridle. Both work pressures and home responsibilities find you coping not just willingly but almost happily, with not a snort of protest. It makes for greater harmony at home and better performance at work.

2 MARCH: FULL MOON IN VIRGO

Family and the neighbourhood, community affairs will be the focus this quarter, and more or less right through the month. It will also see the successful winding up of some business matters which have been very long delayed. It's a time for ties also, both personal and professional, and most importantly, for religion and prayer, philosophy and meditation. The spiritual aspect of your nature will, in fact, influence the predominant theme of home, family, relationships.

9 MARCH: LAST QUARTER IN SAGITTARIUS

It's the quarter of your own birth sign, and all that you do, feel and think is bound to be specially charged, strengthened, fortified. And now your home is your castle, your bastion against a cruel and demanding world, and your family and loved ones, your raison d'être. No more chafing at the bit when responsibilities on the domestic front have to be fulfilled, or there's extra work involved.

17 MARCH: NEW MOON IN PISCES

It's travel, trips, ties – the three Ts going to form the total of communication, whether physical or emotional. It's definitely people and places for you. If you can't make up your mind about important decisions, delay them. A more favourable time will soon come. Expenses will go through the roof, but you'll have to try to keep from overspending on business, or there could be big trouble.

24 MARCH: FIRST QUARTER IN CANCER

Your prestige, standing in the family circle and society will probably be at an all-time high but there will also be fairly heavy responsibilities. You will have earned the popularity that you enjoy. Also important will be care of pets, dependents, the elderly. Both friends and family not only support you but will also actively participate in all your activities.

31 MARCH: FULL MOON IN LIBRA

Determination and sheer gutsy hard work, even a kind of ruthlessness in chasing goals and targets that are beneficial to you, that's the ticket. At the same time, you have to party, wine and dine, dance and socialize. It may be that the socializing is a means to the same end – self-advancement. But that is the theme for the whole month.

8 APRIL: LAST QUARTER IN CAPRICORN

The determined efforts of last week will begin to show results right now. Perks/promotions/popularity/prestige/pelf – all the five Ps come to you but as a result of the sixth P of personal endeavour. It's your own purposeful work that has made it happen. And the other P of personal relationships will be equally wonderful, especially in terms of family reunions and bonds, special closeness to loved ones.

16 APRIL: NEW MOON IN ARIES

The effect will be felt in the sphere of information technology and computers, metaphysics, cybernetics – all those esoteric new fields that dazzle old fogeys like me. It may give an added edge to your work now and added income to you. Thus, TV, the arts, the print media will be the fields that are greatly successful. It's not a time to let yourself become too cocksure. Read the fine print in contracts and documents and be careful not to lose them while travelling. Follow this hunch of mine!

22 APRIL: FIRST QUARTER IN LEO

Once again, you will be single-minded, strong-minded and focused. And that's saying a lot, because with the essential duality of the Gemini temperament, people of your sign are often vacillating, unable to make up their minds. You will realize that money is important, and accept the need to go out and earn it. Not so much for yourself as for your family, particularly your children if you have them, since you will feel that they need to be looked after specially.

30 APRIL: FULL MOON IN SCORPIO

The rewards are there now, but so also the grinding hard work that you put in to deserve these rewards. You will be truly aware of your responsibilities to your family and to society. It is a time when your conscience, the higher self, the career and provider in you will be completely awakened and will inspire you to great heights – especially intellectual and spiritual.

8 MAY: LAST QUARTER IN AQUARIUS

Health problems may be more than likely. Read the last sentence just above. Of course, the non-astrological reason could be either the neglect that you are prone to, or the hard work you've been putting in. You will need, and get the support of not only your friends and immediate family but of a far larger, in fact, ever-expanding social circle and network.

15 MAY: NEW MOON IN TAURUS

You will want to get more and more things done this week. It's as if you think you're superhuman, and are ready to perform the labours of Hercules. It might be difficult for others to cope with the demands you make on them, and there could even be resentment on their part. Patience and tact will get you far more success than finding fault. This is sage counsel from Ganesha.

22 MAY: FIRST QUARTER IN VIRGO

There will be a let-up from within you, in terms of more time and more willingness to relax, enjoy yourself, let down your guard. And this despite the still gruelling pace of work. You will be closer to your loved ones and children, will try and find time for them, even for visiting friends and neighbours. It's also a propitious time for starting up new ventures or projects.

29 MAY: FULL MOON IN SAGITTARIUS

You are in a new avatar, much more gentle, concerned, caring and not just to loved ones and those near and dear, but to the world at large. That's a very sweeping statement, isn't it? But it's a fact that Ganesha has this as the trend for you. Warmth, bonding, tenderness, togetherness. Travel will not be too smooth.

6 JUNE: LAST QUARTER IN PISCES

You will make that special effort, walk that extra mile to be helpful to the sick, infirm, the young, the elderly – all the helpless ones of your circle. Pets, children, parents, even your spouse/mate, will all be cherished and cared for by you. You may even be tempted to overdo it, even financially, so that there is both a scarcity of money and maybe bad health to deal with. So, try to strike a balance, advises Ganesha.

13 JUNE: NEW MOON IN GEMINI

It's your higher self, your other-worldly, spiritual side that dominates now. This is not to say that you abandon the world and go off to the forests on sanyas. Far from it. Family and loved ones find you warm and affectionately caring, but this will be one aspect. Personally, you're after a different kind of fulfilment and march to a different drummer.

20 JUNE: FIRST QUARTER IN VIRGO

A complicated period. There will be some legal wrangles that could be bitterly fought before they are concluded. At the same time, great closeness and pleasure in material ties. Also at the same time, your research/further study/crash course/communication skills require your full concentration. Family, funds and resources will have to be looked after and made safe from risk.

28 JUNE: FULL MOON IN CAPRICORN

The new trend will have money and finance as the main theme, but in terms of long-term financial security and both planning ahead and putting by, investing sensibly. At the same time, the theme of personal growth, mental vision, intellectual attainments, that was there in May, now becomes much stronger, and will remain so for some time. Children's problems may cause worries and tension.

6 JULY: LAST QUARTER IN ARIES

You seem to have finally found the answer how to balance family commitments and responsibilities and your own moneymaking abilities. With harmony restored in your mind, your thoughts turn to love and romance – ready to flirt, dally, make amorous advances! In addition, there could be a brainwave about a lucrative new line of work.

13 JULY: NEW MOON IN CANCER

You are in a rather rash frame of mind, impatient of all snags and delays and are hankering for quick results. It doesn't always happen that way, my friends. There is a time required for every process, and do remember that old saying, 'Haste makes waste.' There could be more danger of losing all that you've achieved. And I mean this not only in 'money' terms, but personally as well.

19 JULY: FIRST QUARTER IN LIBRA

Once again, your career and work will be strongly focused, but there is a change in that you will continue to balance it with home and family and your real self and try to attain harmony between them all. Finances will be important too, but more for family needs than anything else. You, therefore, try to reorient your ambitions and further try to include your own personal religious beliefs.

27 JULY: FULL MOON IN AQUARIUS

Your health is never your strong point, Geminis, and you have been having a lot of stress and could have been listless, tired, run down. You will experience, in this new moon, a major upswing and raised energy levels and resistance and stamina! Equally pleasing will be the upward graph in terms of money, perks, gifts, bonus, lucky investments. The money's really good now. In personal relationships, there could be disappointments, problems.

4 AUGUST: LAST QUARTER IN TAURUS

Travel – actual, and also of the spirit – brings gain and also a growth, a development in your personality. Your attitudes will be gentler, less egocentric, more humane and loving. Personal relationships touch heaven right now. Therefore, you will be content and have your sights firmly fixed on the way you envisage your future.

11 AUGUST: NEW MOON IN LEO

Relationships. One word sumps it up totally – children, romantic involvements, parents, in-laws, siblings, relatives. You may get hurt due to some disputes in the family, but lawsuits and legal issues will be resolved easily and in your favour. The other vitally important feature will be the three Cs – contacts, correspondence, communication – which need to be dealt with sensibly and judiciously.

18 AUGUST: FIRST QUARTER IN SCORPIO

After being totally involved with family and extended family, it's now time to look out for yourself and your own ambitions. Domestic and social issues will proceed smoothly, thankfully, so that you can take action for your own interests and benefit. The media, trade, creative arts, even craft-related business, foreign trade, are all favoured and will yield profit. Go for it!

26 AUGUST: FULL MOON IN PISCES

A fresh, new start is what life is all about, for you Geminis. Projects, deals, interests that were in the pipeline, will now get activated, new friendships and alliances will be formed. You will visit excitingly different places, follow new leisure activities, break out of the old and stale mould into a new, very exhilarating sphere.

3 SEPTEMBER: LAST QUARTER IN GEMINI

The monthly trend which set in last week of soaring 'Higher and still higher' for you, like Shelley's skylark, continues. There is, if anything, an add-on. You will not just impress but totally overpower everyone around by the sheer force and charm you radiate. Recognition, awards and rewards, praise and glory are a foregone conclusion. Ganesha is generous.

9 SEPTEMBER: NEW MOON IN VIRGO

The phase extends to this quarter too. You are totally brilliant and impressive at work, to the utter amazement of your totally bemused watchers. I know I love to exaggerate, but this time it's not an exaggeration at all. Just plain, hard fact. Promotions, popularity, perks, prestige, personal interaction and parents.

16 SEPTEMBER: FIRST QUARTER IN SAGITTARIUS

The frenzied joy, achievements, the glory and the applause finally die down. Your mind and spirit are calm, contented, and you're easy to live with yourself. You are grateful, relaxed, and have realized that you can tap your own innate resources for peace, harmony and joy of the soul, and have come well on the way to mastering the art of living, both the pun and otherwise.

25 SEPTEMBER: FULL MOON IN ARIES

Having achieved tangible, visible goals that are appreciated in the material world, your quest is now for higher ones. Peace and being true to yourself and to those you care for, loving and being loved. It's a fine way to be, but with typical Gemini rashness, don't ever think this can last forever without your continued striving to make it happen.

2 OCTOBER: LAST QUARTER IN CANCER

It's functioning in a group, even if it's through a website, that is your special forte now. And the outcome will be wonderful in terms of success. There will be traffic snarl ups on this journey, and challenges too, but you sail through. Nobody and nothing can stop you when you're in search of your own personal space, but the going could get rough in terms of health.

9 OCTOBER: NEW MOON IN LIBRA

Yourself, yourself as the centre of a group, and now yourself in the centre of home and family. The trend has a line of progression in it. Your responsibilities and family will make demands on your time and attention that you cannot deny. So too will your career. It's up to you to balance them both well and happily.

16 OCTOBER: FIRST QUARTER IN CAPRICORN

You will not only realize your own true potential capabilities and skills but also all the doubts and questions about your actions, and their outcome, will now melt away. You will be stronger, more self-reliant even though that can't be said about your actual health. I'm talking now of other strengths: a) career/business/vocation and b) spirituality/religion/faith.

24 OCTOBER: FULL MOON IN TAURUS

You've not only worked hard but sincerely, devoted to the highest objectives of others before self. Time to relax, unwind, pick out some goodies from the bag of life. These could be entertaining and entertainment, parties, socializing, holidays and vacations, or even all of them, if you have managed to grab a fistful! This is the trend for the month.

31 OCTOBER: LAST QUARTER IN LEO

You will realize that discretion and care are essential if you want to put financial troubles behind you and be totally self-sufficient and independent in money matters. You may even want to set up an independent, home-based business/office for this. Also, equally important for you will be your personal journeys of faith, tantra, mantra, prayer and worship. I'm not talking of pilgrimages or visits to holy places so much as meditation, spiritualism as you try to get closer to realization of God.

7 NOVEMBER: NEW MOON IN SCORPIO

A kind of hankering for being alone, like Christ wandering in the desert, will possess you. You may even be full of doubts, despair and questions. These mood swings are part of the Gemini psyche and you feel you require a change of location or scene to make you feel better. Travel or weekend trips are likely. So also, working for the community concerns about global environment, for society and for human welfare.

15 NOVEMBER: FIRST QUARTER IN AQUARIUS

There will not only be a total, but very visible and definite change in your attitude after the new moon. Your self-doubts, worries may not disappear but they will certainly be set at rest, and the good thing is that the change comes from within. Family and work demands will be tackled with determination and tact, so that you get quick and pleasing results.

23 NOVEMBER: FULL MOON IN GEMINI

In this new mood of squaring up to reality, you will focus firmly on your family, loved ones and friends, and be prepared to go all out for them. Your social and philanthropic concerns, work for charity, and larger causes too. You will have the insight and perception to be able to foresee trends for the future and adjust your own activities accordingly.

30 NOVEMBER: LAST QUARTER IN VIRGO

You're ready for action, if it means starting the process of change. But you realize the need to do so gradually, not totally upset the apple cart. You will also realize that a certain steadiness helps relationships and will try hard to maintain it. Money will be important in terms of planning budgets for home and office.

7 DECEMBER: NEW MOON IN SAGITTARIUS

Both your career and your social life show an upward slant, like the last few overs shown on a graph in a One-day cricket match. You will be able to combine work and recreation, home affairs and work demands, in short, business and pleasure. You will be making, or at least weighing up, decisions that could affect your future and your family.

15 DECEMBER: FIRST QUARTER IN PISCES

A tremendously busy, even fraught, phase starts. And you'll be busy in your every possible way, work, socializing, family affairs and functions, even some secret negotiations and/or politics, if that way inclined. In fact, you'll have to make a conscious effort to relax and rest or there could be a total burnout. Financial jugglery or at least rethinking of it will also be part of this activity, as you think of new ways, to add to your income, balance the budget, and save for the future.

22 DECEMBER: FULL MOON IN CANCER

Major opportunities for gain started coming your way from the end of October. Finances will be good – legacies, inheritances, gifts and windfalls! Great joy in family life, in social interaction. The year ends with a joyous note, with perhaps a stroke of luck too, in the last few days of the years, through the great power of Ganesha.

29 DECEMBER: LAST QUARTER IN LIBRA

Bonds, ties, partnerships, relationships, links – that is what Ganesha sees for you as the old year gives rise to the new. Communication is the name of the game – it may range from email, net surfing, to just a platonic kiss on the cheek. I'm an inveterate romantic at heart, so I think I'd prefer the kiss to being told 'You've got mail'. And I'm telling you I'm not kidding too much.

Achievements 2018

By the grace of Lord Ganesh, my son Nastur found patrons in Shri Raj Kumar Jatia and his son, Shri Adarsh Jatia, the owners of Four Seasons, Mumbai, and Provenance Four Seasons Private Residences. May patience and hard work take my son to the top of the world where Shri Raj Kumar Jatia stands like a shining star. Nastur was graciously invited by the noble business tycoon, Byram Avari, of Avari Group of Hotels, Karachi, and his wife, Goshpi Avari, to attend their fiftieth wedding anniversary.

I bless prosperity upon Prayush Poddar, his father and his family. May his company, AMP Universal Realty Pvt. Ltd, prosper. He has been like a son to me.

May the grace of Lord Ganesha bless Police Commissioner Anupam Singh Gehlot of Rajkot. He has always stood by my family, in good times and bad. Peace and prosperity prevail in Rajkot because of his sincere efforts.

BJP National vice-president and Rajya Sabha member, Vinay Sahasrabuddhe is a very fine and noble gentleman. He was gracious enough to arrange a meeting with Maharashtra chief minister Devendra Fadnavis, who was dynamic and touched by the divine.

Body Language

Ganesha believed astrology to be all about behaviour, relationships and how to handle them. Therefore, the guidelines given below should help you to understand yourself and others. Any information that adds to the knowledge of oneself is always welcome. Here are some examples of body language and its possible interpretations:

POSITIVE VIBES

- Open arms and hands: open and receptive
- Leaning forward: interested in conversation

- Smiling or attempting to be humorous: friendly
- Eye contact with occasional, natural breaks in the stare: focused and curious
- Nodding while listening: attentive and alert
- Open palms: approachable and trusting
- Gesturing with hands while talking: genuinely involved in the conversation
- Upright shoulders: positivity

NEGATIVE VIBES

- Crossed arms and/or legs: closed off, defensive, reserved or suspicious
- Standing with hands inside the pockets: unsure or suspicious
- Fidgeting, running one's tongue along one's teeth, playing with hair

or jewellery or tapping feet: nervous and/or bored

- Lack of eye contact or staring too intently and unblinkingly: untrustworthy
- Leaning back: uncomfortable
- Clasping hands behind the head while leaning back: seeking power
- Drooping shoulders: unsure

Colours of Life

Ganesha believes that life is like a rainbow. Life is like nature, full of abundance and variety. The best part of it is you can actually experiment with the colours given below and have fun. Here, we combine abundance and a variety of colours for joy, use, experience.

- **Energetic:** Red
- **Sporty:** Red, orange
- **Exuberant:** Orange
- **Active:** Orange, yellow
- **Modern:** Yellow

- **Invigorating:** Green, yellow
- **Sunny:** Green, yellow
- **Fresh:** Green
- **Luminous:** Blue, Green
- **Hypnotic:** Blue
- **Regal:** Blue, violet
- **Exotic:** Violet
- **Playful:** Red, orange, violet, yellow
- **Vibrant:** Green, red

(Your astrologer admits that this colour system is *not* his own.)

Important Dates

I have always believed that the fear of failure has never led to advancement of knowledge. These dates and directions may differ from the various trends and forecasts mentioned elsewhere in the book. A different direction is being pursued here. This is a totally different ball game. This is to be taken as an experiment on a mass scale with the readers themselves as guinea pigs (willingly, I hope).

Please remember, as a rule, your birth month and the seventh month from it (including itself) will be hectic. For example, if your birth month is March, the seventh from it will be September. There will be tremendous franticness in both these months.

January: 3–4,8–9, 13–14, 17–8, 21–22, 25–27, 30–31

February: 1, 4–6, 9–10, 13–15, 18–19, 22–23, 27–28 (February is the time for planning the future)

March: 3–4, 8–9, 12–13, 16–18, 21–22, 25–27, 30–31

April: 4–5, 8–9, 12–13,17–18, 21–23, 26–28

May: 5–6, 9–11, 14–15, 19–20 24–25, 28–30

June: 2–3, 6–7, 10–11, 15–16, 20–21, 25–26, 29–30 (June will be synonymous with joy)

July: 3–4, 7–9, 12–14, 17–19, 22–23, 27–28, 31

August: 1, 4–5, 8–10, 13–15, 18–20, 23–24, 27–28, 30–31

September: 5–6, 10–11, 15–16, 19–20, 23–24, 27–29

October: 2–3, 7–8, 12–13, 16–17, 21–22, 25–26, 29–31, (children and ideas may take up your time and energy)

November: 3–5, 8–9, 13–14, 17–18, 21–22, 26–27

December: 1–2, 6–7, 10–11, 14–15, 18–20, 23–24, 28–29

Special Note: From the number of stars in this month you clever, nibble-witted Geminis will find August to be pivotal for contacts, contracts, relationships, favours, and obligations. Attachments and ties made around or after June will run into the next year and may last your whole life.

Secret of Life

Ganesha (whom you may refer to as Allah/Christ/Zoroaster or by any other name) is the ignition key of life's car. To start and launch in the name of Ganesha is to assure success and glory. The power, the dazzling light to see visions, have prophetic dreams, and are all bestowed upon us by Ganesha.

Ganesha says the secret of life is in the ability to change with the changing times. In other words, it is the ability to adapt and adjust to situations, conditions, surroundings, climate change, relationships, and science and technology. His second secret is to keep an open mind. Others are most welcome to their own opinion. The third and final secret is to be true to yourself.

Success Secret of No. 17

Ganesha says the secret of life and astrology is to 'Observe! Observe! Observe!' Angela Merkel of Germany, our own Narendra Modi, former US first lady Michelle Obama, and Muhammad Ali, the world's greatest boxer, were all born on the seventeenth days of their birth months. Here is a picture of the tarot card of number seventeen, called the 'Star'. We can see a lady pouring water on the Earth and providing nourishment. To me the lady is the symbol of the great feminine principle which rules the entire world. There are seven stars in the card. As we all know, seven is the mystical number of spirituality, growth and development.

Narendra Modi, 17 September

Michelle Obama, 17 January

Angela Merkel, 17 July

Muhammad Ali, 17 January

To observe is to see completely and carefully. If you observe the above, you will find that all these four individuals are born on the seventeenth. Secondly, the first alphabet of either the first name or the surname in each case is 'M'. The tarot card points towards a great and powerful destiny. Therefore, for all these reasons I believe that the number seventeen and the letter 'M' go with greatness and glory. Yes, I agree that it may not hold true for all the persons born on the seventeenth of various months. I am open-minded.

Is it but a coincidence or is it fate and destiny? I leave it to you to decide.

World Horoscope 2018

Ganesha says cooking is an art. The challenge lies in the ever-changing nature of the ingredients, the temperature, the flavour, the aroma and the very style of cooking.

The ingredients are: artificial intelligence; healing broken bodies, mind, and spirit (most important); managerial skills of a high order; immense strides in medicine and specially brain power; space travel; robots; biopharmaceuticals; origin of life; God vs technology; climate change; and finally the marriage of technology and humanity.

Let me put it in very simple terms. The years from 2018 to 2020 will have both revolution and evolution. Change is the only constant law of nature. Not only will we survive, we will also prevail. The planets responsible for this constant change in direction are Jupiter, Saturn and Pluto. Jupiter means prosperity, Saturn means inevitable changes and Pluto means drastic and unavoidable situations and effects. These three planets are the trio of the cardinal, ambitious, ruthless sign of duty and responsibility: Capricorn. In short, Capricorn is the father who uses a big stick for others but unhappily not for himself. That is the comedy and the tragedy of the Capricorn sign.

As I have said earlier, this is not the right time for Donald Trump. His world view is one that is corrupted by imagination, illusion and, sometimes, hallucination. The Capricorn North Korean President Kim Jong-un will face terrible times and will be completely defeated in the end by fate. Vladimir Putin of Russia and Theresa May of the UK will find it very difficult to hold on to power. Angela Merkel of Germany is simply wonderful and effective. There is a distinct possibility of a settlement or an understanding between the Jews and the Muslims in 2018 itself. God bless them both. Changes in the regimes in Pakistan and the UK appear certain. In the words of Paul Brenton, 'There is peace behind the tumult, goodness behind the evil, happiness behind the agony.' Nobody has a monopoly over truth, love, justice, mercy, kindness and happiness.

India is certainly tolerant up to a certain extent, but it would be wise, practical and necessary to be much more tolerant and far less rigid and orthodox. Water recycling and the treatment of sewage will be a big changer for our country in 2018 and 2019. It will lead to happiness. I say this in all humility and love for Bharat Mata as I am her child. I certainly bow my head at the feet of Bharat Mata. India comes under the planet of Saturn causing changes that are radical, effective, certain. Our Narendra Modi will hold his own against the world. But India will undergo numerous changes, a few of them could be painful but are necessary in the bigger scheme of events. Not religion but responsibility, duty and development will be the three salient features of India in the coming years.

To be happy we must keep an open mind. Perhaps, I say perhaps the best years will be 2018 and 2021. The year 2021 is most certainly the one when science and technology reign supreme and change the very fabric and direction of all of us. Possibly this is the greatest prediction your humble Ganesha devotee will ever make.

Salute and Tribute

A salute and tribute to the following people:

- Gujarat chief minister Vijay Rupani, in whom I saw a perfect balance in the lines of fate, head and heart on his palms. A great heart and a finely tuned mind.
- Philanthropist and naturalist Firdoz Khambhatta, a dangerously handsome, sharp and brilliant man.
- The lovely Meher Medora, firm of purpose and understanding and sympathetic of heart.

- Aravind Mothi and his sister, Anu Mothi, for offering to make a documentary on my life.
- Hotelier Raj Kumar Jatia for his hospitality and courtesy.
- Behram Mehta for his business acumen fused with immense humility and humanity.
- Jay Shah, son of BJP president Amit Shah, for coming to my house and seeking the blessings of all the mighty spirits and energies of each and every religion.
- The very cultured, civilized, and well-informed education minister of Gujarat, Shri Bhupendra Chudasma for his wisdom as well as his faith in Ganesha.
- Usha Nair, Dr Sunny Shah, Nashit Afroze and their team at the International Human Rights Council for services rendered to NGOs all

over the world. I was very humbled to receive a trophy from them, one I shall always treasure.

- Prince Lakshyaraj of Udaipur for his constant endeavour to help thousands of people through education, NGOs and by example for leading an exemplary life.
- My personal blessings by calling upon all the energies of the world to bless my adopted son Chirag and his fiancée Nikita. They are gems.
- I bow very humbly to my guru, Vashishth Mehta, for coaching me across the path of astrology and spirituality.
- Kudos to Neeraj Bajaj, the son of my late friend and patron Ramkrishna Bajaj, and Dadi Mistry for helping the needy, the weak and the helpless in every possible way. Both are truly magnanimous people.

- Raja Vikram Singh of Jambughoda for his humour and resounding laughter. No wonder his Jambughoda resort is doing immensely well.
- Just as this book is going to press, I met Shiroy and his fiancée, Avasti. Avasti specializes in fashion. Shiroy is an absolute gentleman.
- Lastly, I salute and pay my tribute to all those who seek and serve the cause of peace and goodwill to humanity. To me this is certainly the final word.

About the Author

Born on 11 July 1931, Bejan Daruwalla lives with his wife and their three children. Now, eighty-six years old, he is regarded as one of the hundred greatest astrologers of the last century, as acknowledged by *The Millennium Book of Prophecy* (HarperCollins), having accurately predicted the electoral victory of Narendra Modi at the Kanoria Art Centre, Ahmedabad, on 29 March 2012. Bejan featured on *Hard Talk India* on BBC in August 1999. On 10 December 2010, Bejan was featured in *The Job: Corporate Astrologer* in London's *Financial Times*. Bejan was also awarded the Dr Babasaheb Ambedkar Noble Award on 19 April 2017. Giving Bejan more joy and material achievement was shaking hands with His Holiness the Dalai Lama in December 2013, a moment unforgotten and overwhelming. Bejan has one firm belief: tolerance. He believes everyone has the right to their own ideas and opinions; the perspective of others, even and especially if it differs from one's own, must always be respected.

Important Announcement

Our Ganesha devotee Bejan Daruwalla has moved from Mumbai to Ahmedabad. His Ahmedabad address is:

Bejan Daruwalla
Astrologer and Columnist
C/o Nastur Daruwalla
A-5, Spectrum Towers
Opposite Police Stadium
Shahibag
Ahmedabad 380004
India

Telephone

079-32954387

09825470377

08141234275

Email

info@bejandaruwalla.com

bejandaruwalla@rediffmail.com

Website: www.bejandaruwalla.com